Copyright © Desirae Endres

All rights reserved. No part of this publication may be reproduced, distributed, or transmitted in any form or by any means, including photocopying, recording, or other electronic or mechanical methods, without the prior written permission of the publisher, except in the case of brief quotations embodied in critical reviews and certain other noncommerical uses permitted by copyright law. For permission requests, write to the publisher at hi@desiraeendres.com

Cover design by Desirae Endres

First edition printed 2019

desiraeendres.com

simple morning lists

these lists belong to: _____

Introduction

Mornings have changed my life.

I know some people roll their eyes at the thought of a morning routine. How could there ever be enough time for the typical person that has a full time job, maybe kids, and definitely a lot on their plate? If this is something you want, my suggestion is always to start small. If you can wake up 5, 10, or 20 minutes earlier and spend time setting up your day, I can almost guarantee you'll feel a difference.

The reason? Why in the world would we give up extra minutes of precious sleep? Because if we want to live a purposeful life, we won't just stumble upon it. If we want to live intentionally, we have to set up our days intentionally. It's hard to make that happen when we're taking care of everyone else or rushing out the door. A peaceful morning routine won't make your days perfect, but I'd say if you start with peace, quiet, gratitude, or whatever else you intentionally want to start with, you'll be able to lean on that peace and intention you started with throughout the rest of your day.

I've done a lot of different things in the morning, and I believe your morning routine should be specific to you and what matters to you. When it comes down to it, I don't think there is one right way to start your morning, but I do think that it's important to spend time in the morning setting your day up with intention.

I've created this journal because these are the lists that have transformed my life, little by little, as I've made them each morning. I believe each list you will make in this journal will help transform your life, too.

The Lists

The lists on these pages are here to help you let go of what you don't have control of or what you don't need to be holding on to, get grateful for what you have, and remind yourself of what's most important and where you're headed.

As I've worked creatively over this past year as a podcaster and content creator, my main goal has always been to help women make room for what matters to them. On my podcast, I talk about minimalism a lot, and how it has helped me make room for what matters in my own life. However, I also believe that simply carving out time in the mornings before the rest of my house wakes up has contributed tremendously to my ability to live a life focused on my priorities. It has given me the space I need to reflect and set up my days so that I'm focused on what is most important.

As I've focused on gratitude during these morning times, I've also realized that in so many ways, it is the key to contentment. I think we all would like to be content and happy with our lives, and honestly, that starts by opening our eyes to the good that's around us.

Let's talk about how we can do that every morning by making some simple lists.

List 1: It starts with letting go.

There are so many voices telling us that we should make lists that help us remind ourselves of our goals, chase our dreams, and manifest them into being. I'm not saying that's wrong and I think there is something to that. But I think we can sometimes become self focused when that's all we do.

I was in a busy work season when I was feeling a need for a new list in the morning. At the time, I was writing an affirmations list to help remind myself of the goals I was headed towards and who I wanted to be. I would always add a quick gratitude list as well before I started working. Over time, I was starting to feel anxious, even after I'd write these lists.

I was striving. I was believing that struggling to fight for who I wanted to be and the life I wanted was the right way to spend my days. I was feeling overwhelmed and the progression of the lists I was making each morning seemed to be adding to this mindset that I needed to be fighting for something.

On a particularly mentally exhausting day, I remembered words I heard from author Jess Connolly on a podcast (The Happy Hour Podcast) years ago. She simply said that she started to "take herself out of the running" of being "the best." The day I was reminded of these words, I started to make a surrender list.

Affirmations are great, and that's why there is space for them each day in this journal. It's how we approach them that makes all the difference. Before we remind ourselves of who we want to be and the things we want to accomplish, we have to let go.

We have to surrender negative mindsets, or something we were caught up on the day before, or situations that are out of our control. We have to surrender former versions of ourselves, or the versions of ourselves we keep wishing we could be. We have to surrender whatever expectations we are putting on ourselves each day that are causing us to strive.

Some things I surrender each day? Being "the best" at my job (I'd rather just do the best I can than participate in this invisible competition). Being the perfect mom. Keeping the house perfectly tidy. The list goes on.

When I surrender these things, it helps me pursue excellence in these areas of my life without the silent competition, without the fight, without the scarcity mindset, and without the fear. Instead, I walk towards the best version of myself in these areas with a mindset of abundance and a belief that I am able to become the version of myself I need to be for this day. I move forward with the belief that I am already enough. My hope is that creating a surrender list will help you do the same.

List 2: Get grateful.

I'll keep this simple because I think the power of gratitude is pretty widely accepted. I have found that the key to getting content with the life right in front of me has a lot to do with opening my eyes to the good stuff. A gratitude practice helps us do that.

The most simple way to start a gratitude practice is through a short gratitude list. I haven't included numbered lines in this journal because you can write as much as you want or need in the lines provided, but I typically write down three to five things I'm grateful for each morning.

Since I do this in the mornings, I lean on my experience from the previous day. I also meditate on what is happening in the moment. I will say that "hot coffee in a quiet room" shows up on my list from time to time.

Be specific. What can you give thanks for? If you can't think of anything, just look around you. I know it sounds cliche, but there is truly so much to be grateful for.

Gratitude lists have helped me create other gratitude practices in my everyday life, such as an in the moment gratitude shift. When I create a gratitude list in the morning, and later in the day something unfavorable happens that would normally send me into a negative spiral, I can often shift my brain to be grateful for what is going right. Starting the day with gratitude sets us up for a day focused on the good stuff.

List 3: What's your purpose?

Before you begin this journal, I want you to reflect on your purpose. What is your overall mission in life? What do you care most about? Where do you find deep purpose and satisfaction each day?

It might involve caring for your family, your work, or it may be faith related. Maybe it's all of these things weaved into one central mission. Maybe you'll have a purpose statement for your work and your family, separately.

Your purpose statement can change as life changes, but dig deep for something that is lasting - something that matters deeply to you, to the core of who you are and what you care most about. You can brainstorm it and write it down on the lines below. Remember, this doesn't need to be perfectly worded or profound in any way. Your purpose statement is just for you to see and reflect on daily, and it only needs to mean something to you.

_____
_____
_____
_____

The morning lists have a spot for you to write down your purpose statement each day because this repetition keeps us centered on what is truly most important. It doesn't mean that all of our days will be perfectly focused or balanced around these things. We're simply reminding ourselves as we start the day of what we're here to do and who we're here to be.

I know, It's not technically a list. I know it might sound silly to write the same thing down over and over again, but repetition is key to getting something to really take hold in your heart. Abbreviate it if you'd like, or write it out as bullet points. However you decide to rewrite this statement every day, I think you'll find it to serve you well.

List 4: A reminder of where you're headed.

Affirmations have an important and powerful place in our morning lists. There is power in speaking positive words over yourself. There is power in speaking your dreams over yourself.

To me, affirmations aren't about manifesting something into being. It's okay if that's what they are about for you, but I wanted to share my heart on this.

I personally see them as a reminder each day of where I'm headed, what my goals are, and who I want to be in that day. I even pray over them. Of course, use affirmations however you wish and in whatever way fits into your values and belief system.

I suggest starting with a list right now. Write "I am" statements to start. Anything from the person you want to be in this day (one of mine is "I am a patient and gentle mother,") to big dreams you might have ("Our family is debt free" has been a simple one of mine this year.)

It can be career related, overall dreams you have as a person, or even dreams you have for your family. Maybe it's about a place you want to live, something you want to be able to do for a family member, a career change you want to make some day, etc. The possibilities are endless.

Affirmations give our hopes & dreams legs- dreams of who we want to be today and who we want to be years from now. They take something that we just "wish" could happen and they start to make it more realistic in our minds. When these dreams become real to us, we're more likely to live them out by taking steps in the direction we hope to be heading.

Starting our mornings with these statements remind us where we're headed and who we want to be before we start our day. Write a list here to start. Again, start with writing out statements of who you want to be, what you dream of doing, etc. in the present tense. Each day you can write these same affirmations or change them from day to day. It's really up to you.

_____
_____
_____
_____
_____
_____
_____

List 5: What is most important for today?

Nothing revolutionary here- just a little twist on your to do list. This journal isn't meant to be your planner, but rather a companion for your mornings. I believe planning is an important part of the morning, so I suggest you do that in whatever way works for you. This last piece to the morning lists is meant to get you started.

It's kind of like a to do list, but hyper focused on the *one thing* (or maybe two to three at the very most) that you can today to feel most accomplished. This is the most important thing to put your focus on for the day.

Maybe on a Monday this one, most important task looks like simply getting your house back together after a busy weekend. Maybe on a Wednesday it looks like writing a chapter of your book that you've dreamt of writing for years. Maybe on a Saturday it looks like a baking project you've been wanting to do with your kids. It can be big or small- what is it that you want to focus on absolutely getting done today?

If and when you accomplish this thing- I want you to lay down on your pillow that night and feel like you've done enough. It doesn't matter that there were 14 other things on your list- you focused on the one most important thing to accomplish and that's enough for today.

Even if you didn't do this thing, of course, you are enough- I'd say it to you a million times if I could. Your worth is never in your productivity or your checked off boxes on your to do list. But we are here to do good work, so let's at least remind ourselves of what we'd like to focus on today, try our best to make that happen, and give ourselves grace when life happens and something gets in the way.

Some final notes about the lists.

These lists can take five minutes. They can also take 20, or even more. It's up to you, really. Some days it takes me a long time to wake up and reflect on these things. Other days, I only have five minutes and that is all I take. Regardless, when I start my mornings with them, it's always better than when I whisk myself into my day without them.

I've also included space for more. For your thoughts. For longer lists. For journaling. For nothing at all. For whatever you'd like to use it for. Each day, there's an entire page dedicated to whatever you want or need. Some days I journal, some days I make a longer to do list here, but either way, I like the extra space, and I hope you do, too. I encourage deeper journaling or reflecting in this space any day you can make time for it.

On Waking Up Early

Of course, you can make these lists anytime of the day. Have a few minutes of peace once you get the kids off to school and before you're off to work? Perfect! More of a night owl? Try writing them in the evening. I suggest mornings simply because I think there's something a little magical to reflecting on what matters as we start the day, but everyone is different.

If you do want time for yourself in the morning, but you can't seem to figure out how to wake yourself up early enough, I have a few tips on what has worked for me. I've never been able to follow a routine until about two years ago, and certainly not a morning routine that required waking up early enough for it. Just know that these tips aren't coming from a naturally born morning person.

Before we get to the tips, let's talk a bit about the *why* of mornings. There is plenty of research you can find that will cite study after study about how early risers are more successful, healthier, happier, and the list goes on.

I personally think the benefits are simple: When you wake up early, you are adding time to your day. No, you aren't literally adding another hour to your 24 hours that you get, but you're adding time to your waking hours in a productive way.

You could argue that staying up an hour later can do the same thing, and maybe it can. I think it is more likely that we would use our extra hour in the morning intentionally than we would at night. It's easy to stay up an hour later and scroll on our phones or watch another Netflix show. If we're waking up earlier, though, there's usually resistance involved, and we are much more likely to use that time as we've planned. What could you do with an extra hour in the morning?

I personally wake up about two hours earlier than my daughter, and I start my day with prayer, my morning lists, exercise, and some days, work. If I did not add these hours to my waking time, or if I added them to my evening instead, there is no way I'd have the energy to do these things. I don't really know where exercise could fit, or when I'd be able to plan and set up my day intentionally.

Additionally, when you wake up in the morning to spend time in the quiet, working on yourself, your goals, your faith, setting your day up with intention, or whatever it is you do during this time, you are telling yourself that you are important enough to make yourself a priority. It might be hard, it might take work, and you might have to form a new habit- but you are important, and it is important to create space in your day to take care of yourself- whether that's your body, mind, spirit, or all three.

When I wake up earlier, I start my day more fulfilled, and I am a more patient, motivated, and joyful person throughout the rest of my day. This makes me better for my family and for the work that I do. I believe the same will happen for you if you push past the hard parts of forming this new habit and make it a long term thing.

I've included a fourteen day challenge to help you get started which you'll find at the end of this introduction.

If I've convinced you to wake up earlier, here are some ways to actually make it happen.

First, a note on mindset.

At the beginning of my morning routine "journey," I read *The Miracle Morning* by Hal Elrod, and that absolutely helped. However, The Miracle Morning was a lot to do in one morning and I don't follow that routine anymore. It was a great starting point. One of the things Elrod suggests is to think positive thoughts about your morning. This is such a simple concept, but it worked.

I simply switched my last thoughts of the day from being dread about how early I was going to have to wake up to positive thoughts about how I was going to feel well-rested, and how I was looking forward to my time alone in the morning. Mindset can work wonders, and it's a completely free and easy shift you can make by controlling your thoughts a bit.

Second, don't hit snooze.

Okay, I admit that some days I still hit snooze, and sometimes unknowingly. But my daughter sleeps nearby and I can't let my alarm make too much noise, so this has its downside. Since I know I might hit snooze, I simply trick myself and set my alarm earlier than my latest possible wake up time for a good morning routine.

If you're able to, set your alarm on the other side of the room so you have to get out of bed to turn it off. Of course, don't get back into bed after this. Make a habit to push your thoughts to something you're looking forward to for the morning as soon as you hear that alarm.

Set yourself up for a pleasant morning.

For me, taking 15 minutes the night before to tidy up my home as much as possible so I can wake up a little more peacefully makes me even more excited for my mornings. Setting the coffee and waking up to that aroma can help, too. Laying out cozy clothes, setting up your morning lists journal and pen in the right spot...

Whatever works for you to set yourself up in the evening and start to remind yourself that waking up in the morning will be a good experience can help shift your thoughts about mornings to more positive ones.

Affirmations.

If you really want to become a morning person but struggle to do so, you could even write down an affirmation like, "I'm an early riser," or "I enjoy calm, peaceful, purposeful mornings," each day in your morning lists until you get the habit down.

Go to bed earlier.

Do your best to prioritize your sleep by going to bed earlier if you can. Try it in increments. Go to bed 15 minutes earlier tonight, and then tomorrow, another 15 minutes, and so on, until you find a good bedtime that works for you.

It's not about perfection- but it is about repetition.

You probably won't become a morning person just by waking up earlier every once in a while. You'll become a morning person by waking up even when it feels hard, day after day. Remember this: It only feels hard for a few minutes. Once you've got a warm drink and you are beginning your routine, you'll feel a whole lot happier about your early wake time.

Move in the mornings.

This could take some habit building in itself, but I've found that moving in the morning, whether it be walking or a quick workout, can bring positive energy and adrenaline for a more "awake" early morning routine. I have become an even happier morning person since I started making a routine out of moving in the mornings, and sometimes I move even before I do my morning lists. It's worth a shot if you find that you feel groggy throughout your entire morning routine.

A disclaimer: The early wake up time is not for the mother with a newborn.

If you still only sleep in three hour stretches (or less) because you have a new baby and nighttime feedings, this might not be for you. Prioritize sleep whenever you can get it.

Waking up early might not work for you, but that doesn't mean these lists can't work for you. You can write them when you find an extra 5 minutes to breathe and think. You can half-write them. You can write them a couple of times a week.

These lists are meant to work for you in every season, and they'll look different in each season as well. You don't have to have a perfect capacity or amount of time to do them. I do hope you'll take a few minutes for yourself to think and reflect. You'll be better for it when you prioritize yourself for even a short amount of time, and your family will be better for it, too.

A *starting point*.

These lists can be your entire morning routine if you only have a small amount of time, but they are meant to be a starting point to a morning routine that serves you well. Maybe you'll follow with prayer. Maybe you'll build in some morning exercise. Maybe you'll read a book.

Whatever you choose to do, I hope you'll find a rhythm that fills your cup as you start your day, and I hope these lists will be a purposeful starting point for that. I'm always cheering you on.

Take the Challenge

If you're ready to start waking up earlier, I've created a simple 14 day challenge to help you form the habit. Why 14 days? Some sources will say it takes 14 days to build a habit, others 21, and a recent article by habit expert James Clear suggests it actually takes over 2 months, according to science. All of these numbers can overwhelm us and make us feel like we'll never get there.

I've decided on 14 days because this takes us through two weeks of navigating what it feels like to wake up early, working up to a good hour of morning time, and figuring out what works best for us while trying out a new morning routine. Two weeks just feels like a good time frame to make a decision of whether or not early mornings are going to work for your current season.

My big secret to actually following through with a challenge or a new routine? *You've got to just force your way through it*. It's not going to come naturally at first and it is most likely going to be hard, so accept that as a truth and promise yourself you'll do it anyways.

Before you start this challenge, create a why for waking up early. What is going to drive you to get out of bed in the morning when you want to just hit snooze? What deep why can you lean on in those moments? Write it down on the lines below.

_____
_____
_____
_____
_____
_____
_____

The challenge rules.

Step 1: Set a wake up time that is realistic for you. I suggest an hour earlier than your normal. There are two options with how to get there.

Option 1: Rip off the bandaid and start waking up at your desired wake up time from day one. It will feel hard at first, but if you are ready to just dive in, this is the method for you.

Option 2: Start waking up earlier in 15 minute increments each day until you get to the wake up time desired, and keep that wake up time for the rest of the challenge (and ideally, long after the challenge.)

Step 2: Each day, do the following:

1. Wake up and hour earlier (or whatever your chosen wake time is)
2. Drink at least 16 oz of water
3. Complete your morning lists for that day
4. Optional: pray/ meditate
5. Choose one other thing you'd like to do in your morning routine.

Step 3: Document and record how the routine is going for you each day. You can use the notes page to do this in your morning lists. Take a moment to write down how your morning went, what works and what doesn't, to keep track of how the routine is going.

Share your progress in this challenge (or share your lists each day even apart from the challenge) via social media and use the hashtag #simplemorninglists.

Begin.

Begin today. I know, a fresh start always feels great. Starting on a Monday often feels like the right thing to do, or starting with the first of a new month. I challenge you to put aside those "perfect" starting points and just start today, whether it's a Monday or a Wednesday or whatever day it is. There is no better day to start living more intentionally, more present, than today. I believe these lists will help you do that.

Before we begin, though, I do want you to do one thing: Forget. Forget the days you've felt frazzled, purposeless, frustrated, with no strategy to move forward from those feelings. Forget the failures, forget that you may have never succeeded in following a routine that would benefit you. You have the power to do a new thing in yourself, and you can start today. You can follow through on something that's important to you. You are incredibly capable of change. Forget the days when you believed otherwise because today, and everyday, you get a new start.

Throughout the rest of this book, you'll find space to write your lists each day. You'll also find short essays and weekly challenges like this one every seven days. However, these are just markers for a new week and a new focus and they are meant to inspire you. If you miss a day of your lists, you don't have to skip a page or start a new week if you only went through half the week. Use up all 12 weeks even if it takes you 150 days to do so!

Realistically, some days life happens and our routines get away from us and that is one hundred percent okay! The key is just to start back where you left off as soon as possible.

I hope these lists help you grow and change in all the best ways, and I pray they help you focus on what matters most to you, as they've done for me.

Weekly Challenge

Let's start some list-making! Do your best to journal through the morning lists every day this week to start a new habit strong.

DATE:

THINGS I'M SURRENDERING

_____
_____
_____
_____
_____

TODAY I'M GRATEFUL FOR

_____
_____
_____
_____
_____

MY PURPOSE STATEMENT

_____
_____
_____
_____

WHO I'M BECOMING

_____
_____
_____
_____
_____

TODAY'S FOCUS

_____
_____
_____

Space for your thoughts.

DATE:

THINGS I'M SURRENDERING

_____
_____
_____
_____
_____

TODAY I'M GRATEFUL FOR

_____
_____
_____
_____
_____

MY PURPOSE STATEMENT

_____
_____
_____
_____

WHO I'M BECOMING

_____
_____
_____
_____
_____

TODAY'S FOCUS

_____
_____
_____
_____

Space for your thoughts.

DATE:

THINGS I'M SURRENDERING

_____
_____
_____
_____
_____
_____

TODAY I'M GRATEFUL FOR

_____
_____
_____
_____
_____
_____

MY PURPOSE STATEMENT

_____
_____
_____
_____
_____

WHO I'M BECOMING

_____
_____
_____
_____
_____
_____

TODAY'S FOCUS

_____
_____
_____

Space for your thoughts.

DATE:

THINGS I'M SURRENDERING

_____
_____
_____
_____
_____

TODAY I'M GRATEFUL FOR

_____
_____
_____
_____
_____

MY PURPOSE STATEMENT

_____
_____
_____
_____

WHO I'M BECOMING

_____
_____
_____
_____
_____

TODAY'S FOCUS

_____
_____
_____

Space for your thoughts.

DATE:

THINGS I'M SURRENDERING

_____
_____
_____
_____
_____

TODAY I'M GRATEFUL FOR

_____
_____
_____
_____
_____

MY PURPOSE STATEMENT

_____
_____
_____
_____
_____

WHO I'M BECOMING

_____
_____
_____
_____
_____

TODAY'S FOCUS

_____
_____
_____

Space for your thoughts.

DATE:

THINGS I'M SURRENDERING

_____
_____
_____
_____
_____

TODAY I'M GRATEFUL FOR

_____
_____
_____
_____
_____

MY PURPOSE STATEMENT

_____
_____
_____
_____

WHO I'M BECOMING

_____
_____
_____
_____
_____

TODAY'S FOCUS

_____
_____
_____

Space for your thoughts.

DATE:

THINGS I'M SURRENDERING

_____
_____
_____
_____

TODAY I'M GRATEFUL FOR

_____
_____
_____
_____

MY PURPOSE STATEMENT

_____
_____
_____

WHO I'M BECOMING

_____
_____
_____
_____

TODAY'S FOCUS

_____
_____
_____

Space for your thoughts.

Put Down the Heavy Things

I was working like crazy, fitting work into every margin of my day possible, definitely anxious about deadlines I set for myself, and probably on the edge of burnout when I read the words. They said "take yourself out of the running," and they came to me through a simple Instagram post from author and speaker Jess Connolly.

I first heard these words over three years ago from the same author through a podcast. I was in my car and I almost immediately threw my hands up in the air. These words were exactly what I needed to hear. I needed to stop competing.

Competition isn't always a bad thing, but how many invisible competitions are we putting ourselves in each day? Competitions that aren't even real, but feel very real because we're fighting so hard to win them? I'm not even a competitive person, but I realized I was competing in way too many of these invisible competitions for my own good.

At the time I was fighting to get to the top- top podcaster, most present mother, best homemaker, the list goes on. Basically, I was trying to do all the things and I was trying to do them all perfectly. A lot of this striving was coming from comparison, and a lot of it was just coming from pressure that I put on myself.

I knew it was time to put these unrealistic expectations to rest, so I wrote them down. I'm letting go. I'm waving the white flag. Because these un-winnable competitions, they aren't mine to struggle through.

And then there are the other heavy things we hold- the scary things, the stressful things, the things that are out of our control, or even the things that are in our control but we're not sure what to do with them. I started writing them down, too, and in the process, I started slowly letting them go.

Surrender looks like letting go of the burdens we're not meant to hold so we can live lighter. And while I began starting my day with a surrender list out of a deep need to put down some heavy things I couldn't carry anymore, I kept writing it even after my load was a little lighter because I'm prone pick things back up.

I wish I could say that once you let it go, you'll live lighter, you'll walk more joyfully, and you won't pick up the heavy stuff again- but that would be a lie, and I'd rather be honest.

You'll probably pick it back up. You may pick up the same burdens, the same stress, the same anxieties, the same unrealistic expectations, again, later that same day. That's why we write again tomorrow.

Surrender is a grace filled process. It's not part of our morning practice so we can work towards this perfectly whole and light version of ourselves. It's part of our practice so we can live a little lighter as we continue letting go every day. Perfection is not the goal.

Give yourself grace as you keep letting go of the same things, day after day, until one day you find yourself not even thinking to write them anymore because you've truly let go. It may take years to get there, maybe even a lifetime, and that's okay.

The heavy things you are holding aren't yours to hold. Surrender is really about acknowledging that we weren't meant to live life carrying around heavy things, that we can live lighter. And we can walk towards that truth by letting go, daily, of what is weighing us down.

Weekly Challenge

After you write your surrender list each day this week, posture your body differently. Sit with your hands open and facing up, whether you place them in your lap, in the air, wherever feels right for you, and simply sit in silence. Take a few moments to release the things you've written down. I release these things to God as I do this, but this can be accompanied with prayer, meditation, or whatever works for you and your personal beliefs.

DATE:

THINGS I'M SURRENDERING

_____
_____
_____
_____
_____
_____

TODAY I'M GRATEFUL FOR

_____
_____
_____
_____
_____
_____

MY PURPOSE STATEMENT

_____
_____
_____
_____
_____

WHO I'M BECOMING

_____
_____
_____
_____
_____

TODAY'S FOCUS

_____
_____
_____

Space for your thoughts.

DATE:

THINGS I'M SURRENDERING

_____
_____
_____
_____
_____

TODAY I'M GRATEFUL FOR

_____
_____
_____
_____
_____

MY PURPOSE STATEMENT

_____
_____
_____
_____

WHO I'M BECOMING

_____
_____
_____
_____

TODAY'S FOCUS

_____
_____
_____

Space for your thoughts.

DATE:

THINGS I'M SURRENDERING

_____
_____
_____
_____
_____

TODAY I'M GRATEFUL FOR

_____
_____
_____
_____
_____
_____

MY PURPOSE STATEMENT

_____
_____
_____
_____

WHO I'M BECOMING

_____
_____
_____
_____
_____

TODAY'S FOCUS

_____
_____

Space for your thoughts.

DATE:

THINGS I'M SURRENDERING

_____
_____
_____
_____
_____
_____

TODAY I'M GRATEFUL FOR

_____
_____
_____
_____
_____
_____

MY PURPOSE STATEMENT

_____
_____
_____
_____

WHO I'M BECOMING

_____
_____
_____
_____
_____
_____

TODAY'S FOCUS

_____
_____
_____
_____

Space for your thoughts.

DATE:

THINGS I'M SURRENDERING

_____
_____
_____
_____
_____

TODAY I'M GRATEFUL FOR

_____
_____
_____
_____
_____

MY PURPOSE STATEMENT

_____
_____
_____
_____

WHO I'M BECOMING

_____
_____
_____
_____

TODAY'S FOCUS

_____
_____
_____

Space for your thoughts.

DATE:

THINGS I'M SURRENDERING

_____
_____
_____
_____
_____

TODAY I'M GRATEFUL FOR

_____
_____
_____
_____
_____

MY PURPOSE STATEMENT

_____
_____
_____
_____

WHO I'M BECOMING

_____
_____
_____
_____
_____

TODAY'S FOCUS

_____
_____
_____

Space for your thoughts.

DATE:

THINGS I'M SURRENDERING

_____
_____
_____
_____
_____

TODAY I'M GRATEFUL FOR

_____
_____
_____
_____
_____

MY PURPOSE STATEMENT

_____
_____
_____
_____

WHO I'M BECOMING

_____
_____
_____
_____
_____

TODAY'S FOCUS

_____
_____
_____

Space for your thoughts.

What If

What if,
in the midst of all the expectations we put on ourselves,
in the midst of messy, real life,
we took the time to ask ourselves how we really want to live,
what we want our days to be about,
and decided to craft our days that way,
little by little,
'til our life became this beautiful, vibrant thing we love.

What if we did this because we believed we were important,
we believed our days were important,
we believed our life was precious?

What if we took time to work on ourselves.
On learning who we are.
And working towards being fully that person without hesitation.
I think we'd look around more often and see good.
I think we'd live focused on that good
instead of staying focused on the hard stuff,
if we just took the time to believe that life is meant to be beautiful,
filled up with what we love.

What if we focused on actually living this lovely gift of life,
even in the midst of the mess?
Along the way, somehow, we got too serious.
Along the way we forgot to have fun.
We forgot to savor the good things.
So let's savor them, to the point where they happen more often
simply because we see them more often.

Weekly Challenge

This week, work on savoring the beauty in your everyday. The view out the window of a quiet home, the good that you see there, the peace that you feel.

The belly laugh coming from your little one - simply overjoyed by spending time with you.

The aroma of dinner cooking, and the chaos of the background noise - all a gift because you have the means to put food on the plates.

The accomplishment you feel when you've completed an important work task, or something you've been putting off at home. Take time to savor these small things we so often move right past and miss in our everyday lives.

As we start the week, write down a list of everyday joys. You can write it at the end of your day as you've looked for them all day, or simply look around you right now. What beauty is happening right around you in this moment?

Begin to craft your days around those joys, around taking the time to savor them.

This is how a practice of gratitude starts and a life of gratitude and contentment is cultivated- by simply looking around and actually seeing the good that has been there all along.

DATE:

THINGS I'M SURRENDERING

_____
_____
_____
_____
_____

TODAY I'M GRATEFUL FOR

_____
_____
_____
_____
_____

MY PURPOSE STATEMENT

_____
_____
_____
_____

WHO I'M BECOMING

_____
_____
_____
_____
_____

TODAY'S FOCUS

_____
_____
_____

Space for your thoughts.

DATE:

THINGS I'M SURRENDERING

_____
_____
_____
_____
_____

TODAY I'M GRATEFUL FOR

_____
_____
_____
_____
_____

MY PURPOSE STATEMENT

_____
_____
_____
_____

WHO I'M BECOMING

_____
_____
_____
_____
_____

TODAY'S FOCUS

_____
_____
_____
_____

Space for your thoughts.

DATE:

THINGS I'M SURRENDERING

_____
_____
_____
_____
_____
_____

TODAY I'M GRATEFUL FOR

_____
_____
_____
_____
_____
_____

MY PURPOSE STATEMENT

_____
_____
_____
_____
_____

WHO I'M BECOMING

_____
_____
_____
_____
_____

TODAY'S FOCUS

_____
_____
_____
_____

Space for your thoughts.

DATE:

THINGS I'M SURRENDERING

_____
_____
_____
_____
_____

TODAY I'M GRATEFUL FOR

_____
_____
_____
_____
_____

MY PURPOSE STATEMENT

_____
_____
_____
_____
_____

WHO I'M BECOMING

_____
_____
_____
_____
_____

TODAY'S FOCUS

_____
_____
_____

Space for your thoughts.

DATE:

THINGS I'M SURRENDERING

_____
_____
_____
_____
_____
_____

TODAY I'M GRATEFUL FOR

_____
_____
_____
_____
_____
_____

MY PURPOSE STATEMENT

_____
_____
_____
_____
_____
_____

WHO I'M BECOMING

_____
_____
_____
_____
_____
_____

TODAY'S FOCUS

_____
_____
_____
_____

Space for your thoughts.

DATE:

THINGS I'M SURRENDERING

_____
_____
_____
_____
_____

TODAY I'M GRATEFUL FOR

_____
_____
_____
_____
_____

MY PURPOSE STATEMENT

_____
_____
_____

WHO I'M BECOMING

_____
_____
_____
_____
_____

TODAY'S FOCUS

_____
_____
_____

Space for your thoughts.

DATE:

THINGS I'M SURRENDERING

_____
_____
_____
_____
_____

TODAY I'M GRATEFUL FOR

_____
_____
_____
_____
_____

MY PURPOSE STATEMENT

_____
_____
_____
_____

WHO I'M BECOMING

_____
_____
_____
_____
_____

TODAY'S FOCUS

_____
_____
_____

Space for your thoughts.

Don't Forget to Play

When I watch my dad play with my two year old daughter, I am in awe of his ability to play, to be on her level, and to just have fun.

Growing up, my family and I would always say that my dad was forever 12 years old. We'd say it as a joke and in a loving way, but these days I'm realizing that maybe there really is something wise to staying "12 years old" at heart. When we tell ourselves to "grow up" and lose the childlike parts of us, we often can forget how to have fun simultaneously.

My dad, while being 12 years old at heart, has also never really let anything push him from the pace he wants to live. He doesn't often say yes to things he doesn't want to do. He keeps his schedule open when he isn't working so he can spend plenty of time working on projects he enjoys and being with his family. I never realized how rare this was as I was growing up, but now I can look back and really appreciate how present he has always been.

We are obsessed with productivity and obsessed with being busy. Here's the thing- we often think that when we're busy, it means we're living well. But I challenge you to think again- how do you actually feel when you're busy? Do you feel fulfilled? Happy? Or do you feel worn down and tired, like maybe you're missing some things because your pace is too fast to really enjoy anything at all?

You are in control of the pace in which you live. You are in control of what you commit yourself to. You are in control of what you allow your kids to commit to. You are in control of how long your to do list is for the day.

Maybe it's time to trade in the constantly busy days for soulful, slower ones, or at least move a few steps in that direction. Life is meant for living, for enjoying, for savoring, for playing, for being present with our people. It's meant for other important things, too, like work. But somehow so many of us have leaned completely towards work and productivity that we lost the margin for play. I think we get it wrong when we lose our ability to play- when we believe that there are too many things to do that are more important than fun- so much so that we forget to have fun at all.

I'm thankful for the people in my life, my dad being one of them, who have reminded me to slow down and make room for fun, for savoring, for doing things I enjoy simply because they make me happy.

And today, I wanted to give back by reminding you to slow down and have fun, too.

Weekly Challenge

You don't always have to be productive. Keep your to do list smaller, or at least build in time for play. Savor a slower morning. Take something off of the schedule. Do something you've truly been wanting to do.

DATE:

THINGS I'M SURRENDERING

_____
_____
_____
_____
_____
_____

TODAY I'M GRATEFUL FOR

_____
_____
_____
_____
_____
_____

MY PURPOSE STATEMENT

_____
_____
_____
_____

WHO I'M BECOMING

_____
_____
_____
_____
_____
_____

TODAY'S FOCUS

_____
_____
_____

Space for your thoughts.

DATE:

THINGS I'M SURRENDERING

_____
_____
_____
_____
_____
_____

TODAY I'M GRATEFUL FOR

_____
_____
_____
_____
_____
_____

MY PURPOSE STATEMENT

_____
_____
_____
_____
_____

WHO I'M BECOMING

_____
_____
_____
_____
_____
_____

TODAY'S FOCUS

_____
_____
_____
_____

Space for your thoughts.

DATE:

THINGS I'M SURRENDERING

_____
_____
_____
_____
_____

TODAY I'M GRATEFUL FOR

_____
_____
_____
_____
_____

MY PURPOSE STATEMENT

_____
_____
_____
_____

WHO I'M BECOMING

_____
_____
_____
_____
_____

TODAY'S FOCUS

_____
_____
_____

Space for your thoughts.

DATE:

THINGS I'M SURRENDERING

_____
_____
_____
_____
_____

TODAY I'M GRATEFUL FOR

_____
_____
_____
_____
_____

MY PURPOSE STATEMENT

_____
_____
_____
_____

WHO I'M BECOMING

_____
_____
_____
_____

TODAY'S FOCUS

_____
_____
_____

Space for your thoughts.

DATE:

THINGS I'M SURRENDERING

_____
_____
_____
_____
_____
_____

TODAY I'M GRATEFUL FOR

_____
_____
_____
_____
_____
_____

MY PURPOSE STATEMENT

_____
_____
_____
_____
_____

WHO I'M BECOMING

_____
_____
_____
_____
_____
_____

TODAY'S FOCUS

_____
_____
_____
_____

Space for your thoughts.

DATE:

THINGS I'M SURRENDERING

_____
_____
_____
_____
_____

TODAY I'M GRATEFUL FOR

_____
_____
_____
_____
_____

MY PURPOSE STATEMENT

_____
_____
_____

WHO I'M BECOMING

_____
_____
_____
_____
_____

TODAY'S FOCUS

_____
_____
_____

Space for your thoughts.

DATE:

THINGS I'M SURRENDERING

_____
_____
_____
_____
_____

TODAY I'M GRATEFUL FOR

_____
_____
_____
_____
_____

MY PURPOSE STATEMENT

_____
_____
_____

WHO I'M BECOMING

_____
_____
_____
_____
_____

TODAY'S FOCUS

_____
_____
_____

Space for your thoughts.

Chase Joy

On the Monday I'm writing this, it's the perfect storm: Things are out of place. The aftermath of a full weekend can be seen in the mess. Toys are hidden under the entertainment center. Breakfast scraps are still on the table. The sink is full. I let some routines go over the past couple of days and it shows. But today I'm reminding myself of what is important, and that a Monday morning with messes can still be a good morning.

My anxiety levels are up when I wake up to a mess, which is why I have a routine of tidying up each evening. But life happens, and when life happens, sometimes that routine doesn't.

Today I'm reminding myself that's okay. I have to remind myself that where there is living being done, there will always be messes.

Today, I've allowed myself to let my Monday morning messes just be, breathing out the anxiety and enjoying watching my daughter play on her own, making more messes.

I want a lived in, loved in home that feels warm and inviting more than I want one that photographs well for social media. I may have a lot to do today, but I'm choosing joy instead of anxiety. Because if it doesn't all get done, there is always tomorrow.

We don't have to hold it all together. We don't have to do it all. We can let go a little when we need to. We can rest. We can enjoy what's right in front of us instead of hurrying to accomplish every task and keep every routine running smoothly. We can stop chasing perfection and chase joy instead.

Weekly Challenge

Remember that perfection isn't achievable and that being present is much more important than scrambling to do it all and perfect it all. This week, work on letting messes be until a better time to get to them comes. Work on prioritizing peace & people instead of worrying about perfecting your systems and your home.

Making room for what matters in our life can look like creating helpful routines and following them, but it can also look like getting off the hamster wheel you've been spinning on and letting the mess go so you can be a little more present. Life doesn't always look tidy, and that's okay.

Surrender the perfectly tidy home, the perfectly productive work day, the perfectly behaved kids, whatever perfect image is in your head. These unrealistic pictures in our heads do more damage than good.

Let's really spend time and thought on those surrender lists this week- what are you holding on to that you don't need to be? What imaginary competitions are you feeling burdened by? Drop them, friend. They don't have a place in your purposeful days.

DATE:

THINGS I'M SURRENDERING

_____
_____
_____
_____
_____

TODAY I'M GRATEFUL FOR

_____
_____
_____
_____
_____

MY PURPOSE STATEMENT

_____
_____
_____
_____

WHO I'M BECOMING

_____
_____
_____
_____

TODAY'S FOCUS

_____
_____
_____

Space for your thoughts.

DATE:

THINGS I'M SURRENDERING

_____
_____
_____
_____
_____

TODAY I'M GRATEFUL FOR

_____
_____
_____
_____
_____

MY PURPOSE STATEMENT

_____
_____
_____
_____

WHO I'M BECOMING

_____
_____
_____
_____

TODAY'S FOCUS

_____
_____

Space for your thoughts.

DATE:

THINGS I'M SURRENDERING

_____
_____
_____
_____
_____
_____

TODAY I'M GRATEFUL FOR

_____
_____
_____
_____
_____
_____

MY PURPOSE STATEMENT

_____
_____
_____
_____
_____
_____

WHO I'M BECOMING

_____
_____
_____
_____
_____
_____

TODAY'S FOCUS

_____
_____
_____
_____

Space for your thoughts.

DATE:

THINGS I'M SURRENDERING

_____
_____
_____
_____
_____
_____

TODAY I'M GRATEFUL FOR

_____
_____
_____
_____
_____
_____

MY PURPOSE STATEMENT

_____
_____
_____
_____

WHO I'M BECOMING

_____
_____
_____
_____
_____
_____

TODAY'S FOCUS

_____
_____
_____

Space for your thoughts.

DATE:

THINGS I'M SURRENDERING

_____
_____
_____
_____
_____

TODAY I'M GRATEFUL FOR

_____
_____
_____
_____
_____

MY PURPOSE STATEMENT

_____
_____
_____
_____

WHO I'M BECOMING

_____
_____
_____
_____
_____

TODAY'S FOCUS

_____
_____
_____

Space for your thoughts.

DATE:

THINGS I'M SURRENDERING

_____
_____
_____
_____
_____

TODAY I'M GRATEFUL FOR

_____
_____
_____
_____
_____

MY PURPOSE STATEMENT

_____
_____
_____

WHO I'M BECOMING

_____
_____
_____
_____
_____

TODAY'S FOCUS

_____
_____
_____

Space for your thoughts.

DATE:

THINGS I'M SURRENDERING

_____
_____
_____
_____
_____

TODAY I'M GRATEFUL FOR

_____
_____
_____
_____
_____

MY PURPOSE STATEMENT

_____
_____
_____
_____

WHO I'M BECOMING

_____
_____
_____
_____
_____

TODAY'S FOCUS

_____
_____
_____
_____

Space for your thoughts.

Making Time

"I wish I had time." This is a simple phrase we hear, and maybe even say, pretty often. I know I've said it a lot in my lifetime, and when I look back on the times when I said it most, I realize now that I could have had time for whatever it was I wanted to do if I really wanted it.

My husband says it to me all the time, "you'll make time for what you truly care about." I complained I didn't have time for consistent workouts for quite a while, but after my husband preached these words to me, and after I preached them to a bunch of people through my podcast, I realized I was guilty of the same false belief that "I don't have time." I had overcome this excuse in some areas of my life, but I didn't realize I was falling back on it in other areas.

Make time for what you love. Make time for what gives you life. If you can't currently find the time in your day for that thing, maybe you simply need to rearrange your days.

Don't lose yourself in motherhood, or in an overwhelming job, or whatever else consumes you. Instead, remind yourself that the thing you can't stop thinking about- the thing that fills you up? It's important.

My writing, the podcast, everything else I create? I've had a lot of women tell me that it's amazing that I can keep up with it with a toddler at home. But here's the thing, I'm not special. I am not a super productive person. I haven't found some kind of secret. I simply have decided that what I love to do is important and I haven't let that fact be up for negotiation. I've rearranged my day so that it fits.

I do these things in the early mornings, during my daughter's nap, and on the weekends I ask my husband for a few hours so I can make it happen. I do it because I refuse to believe that we're meant to lose who we are because we're just too busy. I refuse to believe that motherhood is about losing who I am. I want my daughter to see that women can be passionate, creative, and deserve to give themselves the time it takes to do so.

I'm grateful for this gift of creativity, of writing, of sharing what I'm learning with others. I want you to do your thing, too. Make something beautiful, something that matters, something that fills you up. Create. Do your thing. Whether it's a thing you share with the world or keep to yourself.

Make time for it, whatever it is, count it as important and essential. Don't let making time for what you love to be up for negotiation.

Weekly Challenge

What do you keep saying you don't have time for but you wish you did? Maybe this is a clue into something you're meant to be creating or doing in your life.

I recently rearranged my mornings to find space for consistently moving my body. I finally decided it was important enough. Whatever your thing is- decide it's important enough. Rearrange your days. Quit something so you can fit it in.

If you really wish you had time for it- start to put it in its rightful place in your life- or at least give it some space in your days to start.

DATE:

THINGS I'M SURRENDERING

_____
_____
_____
_____
_____

TODAY I'M GRATEFUL FOR

_____
_____
_____
_____
_____

MY PURPOSE STATEMENT

_____
_____
_____
_____

WHO I'M BECOMING

_____
_____
_____
_____

TODAY'S FOCUS

_____
_____
_____

Space for your thoughts.

DATE:

THINGS I'M SURRENDERING

_____
_____
_____
_____
_____

TODAY I'M GRATEFUL FOR

_____
_____
_____
_____
_____
_____

MY PURPOSE STATEMENT

_____
_____
_____
_____

WHO I'M BECOMING

_____
_____
_____
_____
_____

TODAY'S FOCUS

_____
_____
_____

Space for your thoughts.

DATE:

THINGS I'M SURRENDERING

_____
_____
_____
_____
_____

TODAY I'M GRATEFUL FOR

_____
_____
_____
_____
_____

MY PURPOSE STATEMENT

_____
_____
_____
_____

WHO I'M BECOMING

_____
_____
_____
_____
_____

TODAY'S FOCUS

_____
_____
_____

Space for your thoughts.

DATE:

THINGS I'M SURRENDERING

_____
_____
_____
_____
_____

TODAY I'M GRATEFUL FOR

_____
_____
_____
_____
_____

MY PURPOSE STATEMENT

_____
_____
_____

WHO I'M BECOMING

_____
_____
_____
_____
_____

TODAY'S FOCUS

_____
_____
_____

Space for your thoughts.

DATE:

THINGS I'M SURRENDERING

_____
_____
_____
_____
_____

TODAY I'M GRATEFUL FOR

_____
_____
_____
_____
_____

MY PURPOSE STATEMENT

_____
_____
_____

WHO I'M BECOMING

_____
_____
_____
_____
_____

TODAY'S FOCUS

_____
_____
_____

Space for your thoughts.

DATE:

THINGS I'M SURRENDERING

_____
_____
_____
_____
_____
_____

TODAY I'M GRATEFUL FOR

_____
_____
_____
_____
_____
_____

MY PURPOSE STATEMENT

_____
_____
_____
_____

WHO I'M BECOMING

_____
_____
_____
_____
_____

TODAY'S FOCUS

_____
_____
_____

Space for your thoughts.

DATE:

THINGS I'M SURRENDERING

_____
_____
_____
_____
_____

TODAY I'M GRATEFUL FOR

_____
_____
_____
_____
_____
_____

MY PURPOSE STATEMENT

_____
_____
_____
_____

WHO I'M BECOMING

_____
_____
_____
_____
_____

TODAY'S FOCUS

_____
_____
_____

Space for your thoughts.

Lighter Life

I talk about lighter life a lot. Sometimes I talk about this in regards to minimalism and decluttering our possessions. But most of the time, it's just about whatever is weighing us down. I've even talked about this concept already in this journal as I've talked about the idea of surrender.

In most circumstances, we can start right now, today, living lighter. I realized this was true after a particularly tiring season, through a decision to blast some music in the kitchen. I usually get a little stressed out about cooking with a toddler on my legs, so this was a time in my day where I'd often feel anxious.

I would find myself in my head a lot and stressed out, especially while cooking, so I put on happy music and I danced. My toddler joined. Everything instantly felt a little lighter, even if only for a moment.

Lighter life for me in that season looked like kitchen dance parties. What would make your life a little lighter, a little fuller, and bring you more joy in this day?

Sometimes I think we complicate it. We worry and fret about everything. We've been given this one, beautiful life, and sometimes I think we just need to simplify it by asking ourselves how we can intentionally choose, each day, to focus on the things that bring us joy. It doesn't look perfect, but when we work towards doing the little things that bring us happiness we're choosing to care for ourselves, which absolutely can make things a little lighter.

Now, when I start to feel stressed, anxious, or heavy, I try to ask myself a few questions to help me move away from those feelings: How can I focus on gratitude instead of becoming anxious? How can I control my emotions a little better? How can I make a spilled glass of water or toddler behavior affect me less?

Though we can't always snap ourselves out of these emotions, I do think we often have more control than we give ourselves credit.

For me, it has been about experiencing the good things in life that are literally right at my fingertips. How can I have more fun with my toddler? How can I create more rhythms and routines in my day that don't only have the purpose of helping me accomplish more, but have a purpose in creating a more happy and fulfilling day?

This is what life has been for me lately. A focus on the good things. A focus on intentionally fostering fun days and a fun life. I tend to believe God wants us to be happy, or at least joy-filled. Most of the time, that happiness and joy is in our control- it's something we must intentionally choose.

It doesn't matter if your beliefs are different than mine- I think we can all agree we don't go about our days hoping to live heavy, burden-filled lives.

No matter if your daily struggles look big or small to an outsider, life can be heavy and hard. But we can choose, in this day, to question how we let that influence us and do our best to start intentionally walking towards lightness, towards happy, towards joy. There are times when we might need outside help to make that happen- I know I often do. It might not be easy, but it is worth the work to get there.

Weekly Challenge

Though our circumstances can make life feel very heavy, how can you choose lighter life this week? What can you do, intentionally, to love your life and enjoy your days more, right in the middle of your current season? Whatever that looks like for you, put it into practice this week.

DATE:

THINGS I'M SURRENDERING

_____
_____
_____
_____
_____

TODAY I'M GRATEFUL FOR

_____
_____
_____
_____
_____

MY PURPOSE STATEMENT

_____
_____
_____

WHO I'M BECOMING

_____
_____
_____
_____
_____

TODAY'S FOCUS

_____
_____
_____

Space for your thoughts.

DATE:

THINGS I'M SURRENDERING

_____
_____
_____
_____
_____

TODAY I'M GRATEFUL FOR

_____
_____
_____
_____
_____

MY PURPOSE STATEMENT

_____
_____
_____
_____

WHO I'M BECOMING

_____
_____
_____
_____
_____

TODAY'S FOCUS

_____
_____
_____

Space for your thoughts.

DATE:

THINGS I'M SURRENDERING

_____
_____
_____
_____
_____

TODAY I'M GRATEFUL FOR

_____
_____
_____
_____
_____

MY PURPOSE STATEMENT

_____
_____
_____
_____

WHO I'M BECOMING

_____
_____
_____
_____
_____

TODAY'S FOCUS

_____
_____
_____

Space for your thoughts.

DATE:

THINGS I'M SURRENDERING

_____
_____
_____
_____
_____

TODAY I'M GRATEFUL FOR

_____
_____
_____
_____
_____

MY PURPOSE STATEMENT

_____
_____
_____

WHO I'M BECOMING

_____
_____
_____
_____
_____

TODAY'S FOCUS

_____
_____
_____

Space for your thoughts.

DATE:

THINGS I'M SURRENDERING

_____
_____
_____
_____
_____
_____

TODAY I'M GRATEFUL FOR

_____
_____
_____
_____
_____
_____

MY PURPOSE STATEMENT

_____
_____
_____
_____

WHO I'M BECOMING

_____
_____
_____
_____
_____

TODAY'S FOCUS

_____
_____
_____

Space for your thoughts.

DATE:

THINGS I'M SURRENDERING

_____
_____
_____
_____
_____

TODAY I'M GRATEFUL FOR

_____
_____
_____
_____
_____

MY PURPOSE STATEMENT

_____
_____
_____
_____
_____

WHO I'M BECOMING

_____
_____
_____
_____
_____

TODAY'S FOCUS

_____
_____
_____

Space for your thoughts.

DATE:

THINGS I'M SURRENDERING

_____
_____
_____
_____
_____

TODAY I'M GRATEFUL FOR

_____
_____
_____
_____
_____

MY PURPOSE STATEMENT

_____
_____
_____
_____

WHO I'M BECOMING

_____
_____
_____
_____
_____

TODAY'S FOCUS

_____
_____
_____
_____

Space for your thoughts.

On Small (But Big) Dreams

Is your dream good enough?

I thought of this question the other day as I was at the park with my daughter, snacking together on a park bench. I thought to myself in the moment: I'm living my dream, and this is a picture of it.

I quickly reflected on the fact that many people have asked me that fun question of, "what do you do," and I've hesitated and strung words together to validate that I stay home with my daughter and I create things like podcasts and this book you're holding. I'm not sure why I feel I have to validate it all because when I think about it, I don't really have much concern on what others think of my dream. It's something I've worked for. It's something my family has had to make sacrifices for. Staying at home with my daughter and creating in the spare minutes is my dream right now, and it's a good one.

Our dreams can grow and change and shift. Right now, the dreamy things in life look like cuddles, counting toes, reading aloud, slow days, and creating in the margins. I have other dreams too, but this is the one I'm living, and I'm grateful.

Your dreams and desires are enough. They are worthy, even if they aren't "glamorous." If you're living out something you've dreamed up but you're feeling discontent because our cultures says your dream isn't big enough? Forget that. Look at what you have and be grateful and proud of it.

Today's social media culture can make us feel less than as we compare ourselves to others. Don't let it. Fancy dreams, big money, big names- those things aren't everything. I can't speak from experience, but I'm guessing they can leave you feeling pretty unfulfilled.

It can also leave us unfulfilled if that's the life we're comparing ours to.

It's okay for your dreams to look small or insignificant to others. But don't believe the lie that says they are small. Your dreams are important and worthy, simply for the fact that they are yours.

You don't have to chase fancy dreams. Maybe your dream is to do good work, love your family, and be faithful to the things that matter to you. Maybe those dreams feel small within the context of our culture's messages- but please don't forget that those are pretty world changing dreams.

Weekly Challenge

Do your dreams feel small? Challenge that thought. What do you really care about in life? Our culture often glamorizes bigger and better, but I don't really think those are the most fulfilling things in life.

I challenge you to think of your dreams as big and important even when they feel small and insignificant. How are you living your dream right now? If you're not quite there, how can you move towards it?

We write out our dreams each day as affirmations in these morning lists. Make sure those statements you're writing out are aligned with what truly matters to you.

DATE:

THINGS I'M SURRENDERING

_____
_____
_____
_____
_____
_____

TODAY I'M GRATEFUL FOR

_____
_____
_____
_____
_____
_____

MY PURPOSE STATEMENT

_____
_____
_____
_____

WHO I'M BECOMING

_____
_____
_____
_____
_____

TODAY'S FOCUS

_____
_____
_____

Space for your thoughts.

DATE:

THINGS I'M SURRENDERING

_____
_____
_____
_____
_____
_____

TODAY I'M GRATEFUL FOR

_____
_____
_____
_____
_____
_____

MY PURPOSE STATEMENT

_____
_____
_____

WHO I'M BECOMING

_____
_____
_____
_____
_____
_____

TODAY'S FOCUS

_____
_____
_____

Space for your thoughts.

DATE:

THINGS I'M SURRENDERING

_____
_____
_____
_____
_____

TODAY I'M GRATEFUL FOR

_____
_____
_____
_____
_____

MY PURPOSE STATEMENT

_____
_____
_____
_____

WHO I'M BECOMING

_____
_____
_____
_____
_____

TODAY'S FOCUS

_____
_____
_____

Space for your thoughts.

DATE:

THINGS I'M SURRENDERING

_____
_____
_____
_____
_____

TODAY I'M GRATEFUL FOR

_____
_____
_____
_____
_____

MY PURPOSE STATEMENT

_____
_____
_____

WHO I'M BECOMING

_____
_____
_____
_____
_____

TODAY'S FOCUS

_____
_____
_____

Space for your thoughts.

DATE:

THINGS I'M SURRENDERING

_____
_____
_____
_____
_____

TODAY I'M GRATEFUL FOR

_____
_____
_____
_____
_____

MY PURPOSE STATEMENT

_____
_____
_____
_____

WHO I'M BECOMING

_____
_____
_____
_____
_____

TODAY'S FOCUS

_____
_____
_____

Space for your thoughts.

DATE:

THINGS I'M SURRENDERING

_____
_____
_____
_____
_____

TODAY I'M GRATEFUL FOR

_____
_____
_____
_____
_____

MY PURPOSE STATEMENT

_____
_____
_____

WHO I'M BECOMING

_____
_____
_____
_____
_____

TODAY'S FOCUS

_____
_____
_____

Space for your thoughts.

DATE:

THINGS I'M SURRENDERING

_____
_____
_____
_____
_____
_____

TODAY I'M GRATEFUL FOR

_____
_____
_____
_____
_____
_____

MY PURPOSE STATEMENT

_____
_____
_____
_____

WHO I'M BECOMING

_____
_____
_____
_____
_____

TODAY'S FOCUS

_____
_____
_____

Space for your thoughts.

The More Trap

There's this thing I like to call the more trap. The more trap makes us believe we'll find our worth once we achieve the next goal, check off the next item on our to do list, buy that next home decor item at Target, or live up to that next measure that will make us somehow better or more successful.

The more trap tells us that striving is the way to fulfillment, that we have to struggle and fight towards more to be worthy.

I could go on and on about how this more trap can manifest in every area of our lives, but what I think is most interesting about it is that if you shut down the more trap in one are of life, it will find its way to sneak in somewhere else. When I closed the more trap in my home, in my schedule, and even in some areas of my mindset, it found its way into my work.

The more trap, no matter where it finds you, will bring you some pretty good lies. Lies like, "if I had a nicer car, I'd be more confident," or "if I buy my kids more toys, they'll know I love them," or "I won't be pretty enough unless I lose 10 pounds."

When I found the more trap in my work, it told me lies like "this is impossible to figure out," and "I am not enough," and "I don't have enough time."

When we discover the more trap working in our lives, we have to work to let go of the striving. It can be hard, but it is good and important work.

When we strive, it means we're working tirelessly, we're fighting, we're struggling, on purpose. I'm not saying life is never a struggle or it's never a fight, but I'm saying I don't think we should make it one on purpose.

There is lighter life available when we stop believing that our worth comes from striving for more.

Weekly Challenge

Look at your life. In what areas do you feel tired? Overwhelmed? Burnt out? These are the areas of your life where the more trap might be finding its way in. Most of the time, we don't even realize it's there because it's culturally normal, which means we often don't know how to fight it.

This week, I encourage you to fight it by moving towards less in some way. Sometimes it looks like quitting something, sometimes getting rid of and decluttering physical items, sometimes changing our habits, and sometimes letting go. Almost always, it looks like moving towards less in some small way, because the more trap will have us believing more means more, when in most cases, less is truly more.

DATE:

THINGS I'M SURRENDERING

_____
_____
_____
_____
_____

TODAY I'M GRATEFUL FOR

_____
_____
_____
_____
_____

MY PURPOSE STATEMENT

_____
_____
_____

WHO I'M BECOMING

_____
_____
_____
_____

TODAY'S FOCUS

_____
_____
_____

Space for your thoughts.

DATE:

THINGS I'M SURRENDERING

_____
_____
_____
_____
_____
_____

TODAY I'M GRATEFUL FOR

_____
_____
_____
_____
_____
_____

MY PURPOSE STATEMENT

_____
_____
_____

WHO I'M BECOMING

_____
_____
_____
_____
_____

TODAY'S FOCUS

_____
_____
_____

Space for your thoughts.

DATE:

THINGS I'M SURRENDERING

_____
_____
_____
_____
_____
_____

TODAY I'M GRATEFUL FOR

_____
_____
_____
_____
_____
_____

MY PURPOSE STATEMENT

_____
_____
_____
_____

WHO I'M BECOMING

_____
_____
_____
_____
_____
_____

TODAY'S FOCUS

_____
_____
_____

Space for your thoughts.

DATE:

THINGS I'M SURRENDERING

_____
_____
_____
_____
_____

TODAY I'M GRATEFUL FOR

_____
_____
_____
_____
_____

MY PURPOSE STATEMENT

_____
_____
_____
_____

WHO I'M BECOMING

_____
_____
_____
_____

TODAY'S FOCUS

_____
_____
_____

Space for your thoughts.

DATE:

THINGS I'M SURRENDERING

_____
_____
_____
_____
_____

TODAY I'M GRATEFUL FOR

_____
_____
_____
_____
_____

MY PURPOSE STATEMENT

_____
_____
_____
_____

WHO I'M BECOMING

_____
_____
_____
_____

TODAY'S FOCUS

_____
_____
_____

Space for your thoughts.

DATE:

THINGS I'M SURRENDERING

_____
_____
_____
_____
_____

TODAY I'M GRATEFUL FOR

_____
_____
_____
_____
_____

MY PURPOSE STATEMENT

_____
_____
_____
_____

WHO I'M BECOMING

_____
_____
_____
_____
_____

TODAY'S FOCUS

_____
_____
_____
_____

Space for your thoughts.

DATE:

THINGS I'M SURRENDERING

_____
_____
_____
_____
_____
_____

TODAY I'M GRATEFUL FOR

_____
_____
_____
_____
_____
_____

MY PURPOSE STATEMENT

_____
_____
_____
_____

WHO I'M BECOMING

_____
_____
_____
_____
_____
_____

TODAY'S FOCUS

_____
_____
_____

Space for your thoughts.

Accepting You

I was writing a note to myself the other day, clarifying and reflecting on my mission. This is what came out- as a note to self, but then also as a note to you:

Be you.
The ever-changing, full, unfiltered version of yourself.
Be you without worrying what people will say.
Or at least, keep convincing yourself you're not worried about them,
until it's actually (mostly) true.
Be you until you know who "you" actually are.
Until you're okay with that person-
And not even just okay, but happy, even.
Be you until it becomes easy.
Until it no longer requires work.
Be you until you settle in there.
Until you can retire the mask.
Be you until you no longer have to be reminded to be you.
Be you until you are.

I don't know how to describe this phenomenon that we have to be reminded to be ourselves. Of course, this person, this "true self," becomes hard to uncover underneath the layers of trying to impress, to prove, to win, to be who we think others want us to be.

We are created to be different, beautiful in our own entirely unique ways. Yet, the world can teach us otherwise. Over time, we start to believe that we should find ways to fit in and conform so we'll be liked, that we shouldn't let our true selves be seen because that's too vulnerable. What if we aren't accepted?

There has been this self discovery that has come with my journey to living more intentionally. I've had to dig in deep to what I care about and what's important to me. It hasn't been easy to dig deep enough to clear the dirt of insecurity, the pressure to impress, the fear of not being liked or accepted.

Why is it work to "be you?" Why must we put effort into being ourselves? I think the effort is in moving past what gets in our way of being fully ourselves.

I don't know that we ever get there in this life. Maybe with age, with time, with surrounding ourselves with people that truly love us, with leaning on our faith. Maybe we arrive. Maybe we don't. But I do believe this: We're meant to tell our truth. To use our unique gifts. To live and love in our own unique way.

We can't do that if we're living in fear of being found out- if we're so afraid to be ourselves we don't even know who we truly are.

Keep doing the hard work. Keep peeling back the layers of who you are. Keep actively choosing to love the person you find, and working towards becoming the person you were made to be before everyone else told you who you should be.

Weekly Challenge

Journal about yourself this week. Whether you do it daily or just take some extended time to do so one morning, start to explore who you are, what you love, and what you care about. Some ideas to help you get started: Make a list of things that make you happy, things you love to do, your favorite childhood activities, your talents, your strengths, your weaknesses, what frustrates you, your message, and whatever else you can think of to reflect on who you truly are.

As you work on these lists, work on accepting yourself as you are. Remind yourself of the simple words, "you are enough," as you reflect.

DATE:

THINGS I'M SURRENDERING

_____
_____
_____
_____
_____
_____

TODAY I'M GRATEFUL FOR

_____
_____
_____
_____
_____
_____

MY PURPOSE STATEMENT

_____
_____
_____
_____

WHO I'M BECOMING

_____
_____
_____
_____
_____

TODAY'S FOCUS

_____
_____
_____
_____

Space for your thoughts.

DATE:

THINGS I'M SURRENDERING

_____
_____
_____
_____
_____

TODAY I'M GRATEFUL FOR

_____
_____
_____
_____
_____

MY PURPOSE STATEMENT

_____
_____
_____

WHO I'M BECOMING

_____
_____
_____
_____

TODAY'S FOCUS

_____
_____
_____

Space for your thoughts.

DATE:

THINGS I'M SURRENDERING

_____
_____
_____
_____
_____

TODAY I'M GRATEFUL FOR

_____
_____
_____
_____
_____

MY PURPOSE STATEMENT

_____
_____
_____

WHO I'M BECOMING

_____
_____
_____
_____

TODAY'S FOCUS

_____
_____
_____

Space for your thoughts.

DATE:

THINGS I'M SURRENDERING

_____
_____
_____
_____
_____

TODAY I'M GRATEFUL FOR

_____
_____
_____
_____
_____

MY PURPOSE STATEMENT

_____
_____
_____
_____

WHO I'M BECOMING

_____
_____
_____
_____

TODAY'S FOCUS

_____
_____
_____

Space for your thoughts.

DATE:

THINGS I'M SURRENDERING

_____
_____
_____
_____
_____
_____

TODAY I'M GRATEFUL FOR

_____
_____
_____
_____
_____
_____

MY PURPOSE STATEMENT

_____
_____
_____
_____

WHO I'M BECOMING

_____
_____
_____
_____
_____

TODAY'S FOCUS

_____
_____
_____

Space for your thoughts.

DATE:

THINGS I'M SURRENDERING

_____
_____
_____
_____
_____
_____

TODAY I'M GRATEFUL FOR

_____
_____
_____
_____
_____
_____

MY PURPOSE STATEMENT

_____
_____
_____
_____

WHO I'M BECOMING

_____
_____
_____
_____
_____
_____

TODAY'S FOCUS

_____
_____
_____
_____

Space for your thoughts.

DATE:

THINGS I'M SURRENDERING

_____
_____
_____
_____
_____

TODAY I'M GRATEFUL FOR

_____
_____
_____
_____
_____

MY PURPOSE STATEMENT

_____
_____
_____

WHO I'M BECOMING

_____
_____
_____
_____
_____

TODAY'S FOCUS

_____
_____
_____

Space for your thoughts.

Tired Thursdays

Ever feel a Thursday slump? I've been feeling this for as long as I can remember. When I was a teacher, I used to think this was just a phenomenon teachers experienced. Now that I work part time from home as I stay at home with my toddler, I know it's not just teachers. The Thursday slump is real and no one is safe from it.

By Thursday I'm tired. I'm ready to eat terribly after making healthy choices all week. I'm ready to impulse buy something stupid even though I value living with less and intentional spending habits. By Thursday, I can find myself feeling super insecure. Sometimes I become not-my-favorite version of myself. By Thursday, I can feel like I'm just not enough. Like I must have been some kind of imposter yesterday, when I had it more together, because this messy Thursday version is the real me.

Maybe you don't know what I'm talking about and you think I'm crazy, but here's why I'm saying this- it's not just about Thursdays. It's not just about comparing the tired version of ourselves today to the more put together version of ourselves that existed yesterday, either.

The way we live our lives so connected, so inundated with watching others' lives, can make us look at one another and think everyone else has their life together. We believe the celebrities or bloggers we love to follow are so confident and put together and have their values straight at all times. The people we take advice from, whether an author or someone writing a post on instagram, somehow become the people we start to believe are above us.

We all tend to put our best selves out there and let comparison get the best of us in the process. We often share the good stuff on social media, and maybe we forget to share the hard stuff. Because we're often spending time in our days looking at others' highlight reels and maybe even sharing our own, we can start to believe that we're the only ones who are feeling so messy and disheveled on a

Thursday (or any day).

Here's what is real, and what I have to remind myself: the real me is this Thursday person- this messy, disheveled, tired, insecure person. But the real me is also the yesterday person. The one who, most days, tries to live as intentionally as possible (while still a good dose of messy). The one who holds on to gratitude. The one who is creative and present and loves her people the best she can.

Remember this: we are accepted and loved in full, the Thursday person and the "better" version. We are fully imperfect yet fully enough.

I'm choosing to believe that even Beyonce has a Thursday person version of herself. We're all a little insecure, we're all imperfect, we're all a mess, and we're all enough.

Weekly Challenge

Simply be kind to yourself this week. When you start to feel tired or have a harder time being patient, don't allow your mean-girl inner dialogue to take control. Instead, pause, breathe a little, and find rest where you can- the type of rest that fills you up and truly replenishes you.

Write down a list of the things that bring you that kind of rest so you can reference them for the future.

DATE:

THINGS I'M SURRENDERING

_____
_____
_____
_____
_____

TODAY I'M GRATEFUL FOR

_____
_____
_____
_____
_____

MY PURPOSE STATEMENT

_____
_____
_____

WHO I'M BECOMING

_____
_____
_____
_____

TODAY'S FOCUS

_____
_____
_____

Space for your thoughts.

DATE:

THINGS I'M SURRENDERING

_____
_____
_____
_____
_____

TODAY I'M GRATEFUL FOR

_____
_____
_____
_____
_____

MY PURPOSE STATEMENT

_____
_____
_____

WHO I'M BECOMING

_____
_____
_____
_____
_____

TODAY'S FOCUS

_____
_____
_____

Space for your thoughts.

DATE:

THINGS I'M SURRENDERING

_____
_____
_____
_____
_____

TODAY I'M GRATEFUL FOR

_____
_____
_____
_____
_____

MY PURPOSE STATEMENT

_____
_____
_____
_____

WHO I'M BECOMING

_____
_____
_____
_____
_____

TODAY'S FOCUS

_____
_____
_____

Space for your thoughts.

DATE:

THINGS I'M SURRENDERING

_____
_____
_____
_____
_____
_____

TODAY I'M GRATEFUL FOR

_____
_____
_____
_____
_____
_____

MY PURPOSE STATEMENT

_____
_____
_____
_____

WHO I'M BECOMING

_____
_____
_____
_____
_____

TODAY'S FOCUS

_____
_____
_____

Space for your thoughts.

DATE:

THINGS I'M SURRENDERING

_____
_____
_____
_____
_____
_____

TODAY I'M GRATEFUL FOR

_____
_____
_____
_____
_____
_____

MY PURPOSE STATEMENT

_____
_____
_____
_____

WHO I'M BECOMING

_____
_____
_____
_____
_____

TODAY'S FOCUS

_____
_____
_____
_____

Space for your thoughts.

DATE:

THINGS I'M SURRENDERING

_____
_____
_____
_____
_____
_____

TODAY I'M GRATEFUL FOR

_____
_____
_____
_____
_____
_____

MY PURPOSE STATEMENT

_____
_____
_____

WHO I'M BECOMING

_____
_____
_____
_____
_____

TODAY'S FOCUS

_____
_____
_____

Space for your thoughts.

DATE:

THINGS I'M SURRENDERING

_____
_____
_____
_____
_____
_____

TODAY I'M GRATEFUL FOR

_____
_____
_____
_____
_____
_____

MY PURPOSE STATEMENT

_____
_____
_____
_____

WHO I'M BECOMING

_____
_____
_____
_____
_____

TODAY'S FOCUS

_____
_____
_____
_____

Space for your thoughts.

Speak Life

I catch myself saying really terrible, mean things to myself some days. I've learned to turn myself around in these moments and stop the rude inner dialogue, but it has taken work to get to the point where I have the ability to do this.

I also used to complain a lot and be a pretty negative person, especially around the people closest to me, and I realize now that this mean inner dialogue that I had going on was part of the reason.

Our words hold so much power. This is why bullying is such a real problem- the words we say about others are words they often take to heart and use to define themselves. Maybe that's where our own inner dialogue comes from: words someone once said about us- a time when someone said we weren't enough in one way or another.

We don't have to stay stuck in that dialogue, though. We don't have to keep telling ourselves these negative things. Because our words have such deep power, they also have the power to build us up, as long as we take the time to create a new story to tell ourselves.

My negative inner dialogue doesn't pop up as often these days, and it certainly doesn't hold as much of a grip on me when it does, but it happened again just the other day. The house was a mess and I had some deadlines to meet. I felt disheveled, anxious, and I wasn't being the most patient mother in that moment. As I hurried around my home trying to prepare lunch and maybe clean up a couple of things along the way, I started bullying myself with my own words.

These days, though, when that happens, I've made a habit of catching myself as fast as possible and silencing the negativity. I immediately tell myself to speak life. I tell myself I'm enough. I tell myself I can get it together. I tell myself I'm doing a good job.

I encourage you to start making a habit of speaking life over yourself. It starts with our affirmations lists in the morning, and we can fall back on those positive statements about who we are and who we are becoming later in the day.

We're often encouraged to use our words to build one another up, which is of course a worthy cause. But please don't forget to use your words to build yourself up, too.

Weekly Challenge

How do you talk to yourself? I encourage you to tune in to your inner dialogue this week and pay attention to the things you're telling yourself. If you find it to be negative, take time to craft a new, positive inner dialogue. You may even want to write it down. When you catch yourself in that negative inner dialogue, replace it with the new, life giving, positive dialogue you've written.

DATE:

THINGS I'M SURRENDERING

_____
_____
_____
_____
_____
_____

TODAY I'M GRATEFUL FOR

_____
_____
_____
_____
_____
_____

MY PURPOSE STATEMENT

_____
_____
_____
_____

WHO I'M BECOMING

_____
_____
_____
_____
_____

TODAY'S FOCUS

_____
_____
_____

Space for your thoughts.

DATE:

THINGS I'M SURRENDERING

_____
_____
_____
_____
_____
_____

TODAY I'M GRATEFUL FOR

_____
_____
_____
_____
_____
_____

MY PURPOSE STATEMENT

_____
_____
_____
_____

WHO I'M BECOMING

_____
_____
_____
_____
_____

TODAY'S FOCUS

_____
_____
_____

Space for your thoughts.

DATE:

THINGS I'M SURRENDERING

_____
_____
_____
_____
_____
_____

TODAY I'M GRATEFUL FOR

_____
_____
_____
_____
_____
_____

MY PURPOSE STATEMENT

_____
_____
_____
_____
_____

WHO I'M BECOMING

_____
_____
_____
_____
_____
_____

TODAY'S FOCUS

_____
_____
_____

Space for your thoughts.

DATE:

THINGS I'M SURRENDERING

_____
_____
_____
_____
_____
_____

TODAY I'M GRATEFUL FOR

_____
_____
_____
_____
_____
_____

MY PURPOSE STATEMENT

_____
_____
_____
_____

WHO I'M BECOMING

_____
_____
_____
_____
_____
_____

TODAY'S FOCUS

_____
_____
_____

Space for your thoughts.

DATE:

THINGS I'M SURRENDERING

_____
_____
_____
_____
_____
_____

TODAY I'M GRATEFUL FOR

_____
_____
_____
_____
_____
_____

MY PURPOSE STATEMENT

_____
_____
_____
_____

WHO I'M BECOMING

_____
_____
_____
_____
_____
_____

TODAY'S FOCUS

_____
_____
_____

Space for your thoughts.

DATE:

THINGS I'M SURRENDERING

_____
_____
_____
_____
_____
_____

TODAY I'M GRATEFUL FOR

_____
_____
_____
_____
_____

MY PURPOSE STATEMENT

_____
_____
_____
_____

WHO I'M BECOMING

_____
_____
_____
_____
_____

TODAY'S FOCUS

_____
_____
_____

Space for your thoughts.

DATE:

THINGS I'M SURRENDERING

_____
_____
_____
_____
_____
_____

TODAY I'M GRATEFUL FOR

_____
_____
_____
_____
_____
_____

MY PURPOSE STATEMENT

_____
_____
_____
_____

WHO I'M BECOMING

_____
_____
_____
_____
_____

TODAY'S FOCUS

_____
_____
_____

Space for your thoughts.

Continue the Journey

Congratulations on spending twelve weeks setting up your days well and spending a little bit of time on yourself! I hope you've seen positive change in your life and more intentional days through taking a few minutes in your morning to simply let go, get grateful, and remind yourself where you're headed.

If you want to continue this journey of list-making, find the Simple Morning Lists Journal right where you found it this first time, on amazon.com.

About the Author

Desirae is a mom, wife, host of the top rated podcast, Minimal-ish, and a former classroom teacher turned online educator and work at home mom. Her goal is to give women the tools they need to dive into the version of realistic minimalism that fits their family best, and to live more intentionally, focused on what matters to them.

She believes that God lead her family to minimalism and changed her life through it, and she now feels called her to share her story so other women can experience the freedom of living with less.

She spends her days in Pittsburgh, PA with her toddler, husband, and giant golden doodle pup, enjoying the people she loves and the work she feels called to do.

Find more from Desirae at desiraeendres.com.

Acknowledgements

To Nick: For always reminding me that we make time for what we truly care about.

To Gemma: For bringing me more laughter and joy than I knew existed in this world and for inspiring me to be present and love life more.

References

The Miracle Morning by Hal Elrod
You are the Girl for the Job by Jess Connolly
"How Long Does it Actually Take to Form a New Habit? (Backed by Science)" by James Clear (jamesclear.com/new-habit)

CPSIA information can be obtained
at www.ICGtesting.com
Printed in the USA
BVHW010253020120
568356BV00007B/392/P

9 781700 442260